Condensation

Evaporation

Collection

Groundwood Books / House of Anansi Press
groundwoodbooks.com

Groundwood Books respectfully acknowledges that the land on which
we operate is the Traditional Territory of many Nations, including the
Anishinabeg, the Wendat and the Haudenosaunee. It is also the Treaty
Lands of the Mississaugas of the Credit.

We gratefully acknowledge for their financial support of our publishing
program the Canada Council for the Arts, the Ontario Arts Council and
the Government of Canada.

Canada Council   Conseil des Arts
for the Arts   du Canada

ONTARIO ARTS COUNCIL
CONSEIL DES ARTS DE L'ONTARIO
an Ontario government agency
un organisme du gouvernement de l'Ontario

With the participation of the Government of Canada | Canadä
Avec la participation du gouvernement du Canada

Library and Archives Canada Cataloguing in Publication
Title: City of water / Andrea Curtis ; illustrated by Katy Dockrill.
Names: Curtis, Andrea, author. | Dockrill, Katy, illustrator.
Series: ThinkCities.
Description: Series statement: ThinkCities
Identifiers: Canadiana (print) 20200253484 | Canadiana (ebook)
    20200253492 | ISBN 9781773061443 (hardcover) | ISBN
    9781773061450 (EPUB) | ISBN 9781773064475 (Kindle)
Subjects: LCSH: Municipal water supply—Juvenile literature. | LCSH:
    Water—Juvenile literature.
Classification: LCC TD348 .C87 2021 | DDC j363.6/1—dc23

The illustrations were created with brush and ink on paper,
then finished in Photoshop.
Design by Michael Solomon
Printed and bound in China

For my parents,
who passed on their passion
for the water
— AC

For my parents
— KD

CITY OF WATER

WRITTEN BY
ANDREA CURTIS

ILLUSTRATED BY
KATY DOCKRILL

Groundwood Books
House of Anansi Press
Toronto / Berkeley

RUSHING in underground pipes, meandering through city streams, spraying from grand fountains and twisty little garden hoses — water brings life to our cities. All living things need it to thrive.

Our bodies are around 60 percent water. We can't go more than a few days without drinking it, or we won't survive.

Nearly three-quarters of the earth is also covered by water, though much of it is in the ocean and undrinkable. Some water is frozen in glaciers and ice caps. Less than 1 percent of our planet's water is fresh and readily accessible for drinking.

Still, it's easy *not* to think about water if you live in a city where it flows from the faucet with a mere flick of the wrist.

It's easy to forget that water is a limited resource.

The history of cities begins with water — most urban centers grew up near rivers, lakes or oceans. But as cities expanded, it became necessary to supply residents with drinking water and sanitation systems to get rid of waste.

Some of the earliest cities with such systems were in the Indus Valley, in parts of modern-day Afghanistan, Pakistan and India. As far back as 2500 BCE, in the city of Mohenjo-daro, most people had their own bathing areas and homes were connected to a waste-removal system.

Cities in the vast territory occupied by Ancient Rome (753 BCE to 476 CE) are also known for their water supply and plumbing. The Romans built huge structures called aqueducts (right), some of which still stand today.

Aqueducts acted like artificial streams, transporting water downhill from lakes or rivers using the power of gravity. The Romans also constructed underground tunnels so water could be supplied to homes, businesses and the public baths (left).

Despite these early innovations, many homes in cities around the world did not have indoor plumbing or running water for another 1,500 years. In Britain, the flush toilet was a luxury only for the wealthy well into the 1800s. In the USA, only 1 percent of homes had indoor plumbing by 1920.

Eventually, fear of water-borne illnesses (such as diarrhea, dysentery and cholera) pushed cities to create treatment plants and build massive water systems beneath the streets.

7

8

Today, more than two billion people around the world still do not have access to safe, fresh water at home.

They must spend their days carrying it from a shared well, stream or tank. Women and children are especially burdened with this task. Sometimes the journey is dangerous, and the hours women spend fetching water mean they may not have time to earn money and care for their families. Children may not be able to go to school.

Some people live in cities where the water carries disease or is contaminated.

As the world's population grows, pollution increases and our climate changes, access to clean water is becoming an urgent issue. The United Nations warns that by 2025 half the world will be living in areas that have limited or poor-quality water.

But we can still change this for the better! We can start by learning more about where water comes from, how it gets to our taps and where it goes when it disappears down the drain.

Deep in mountain glaciers, in faraway rivers, lakes and streams, water begins its journey to us.

These water sources and the land around them are called the watershed. Rainfall and melting snow collect in the watershed and drain into larger lakes, oceans and reservoirs.

About 90 percent of the watersheds that provide water for the world's largest cities have been polluted or degraded over the last century. Population growth, the expansion of farms, deforestation and mining have harmed these environments and affected water at the source.

By the time it reaches the city, water is often unsafe and must be cleaned and treated heavily to make it drinkable.

That's why more and more cities are trying to think upstream, beginning the path to clean water by protecting the forests, mountains, lakes, rivers and wetlands where it comes from. Citizens' groups everywhere are monitoring water quality, tracking down polluters and taking them to court, as well as raising awareness in schools and with politicians to preserve and protect their waterways.

Cities such as San Antonio, Texas, and the entire Canadian province of Prince Edward Island pump their water straight from the ground.

Groundwater exists in the spaces between rock and soil, as well as in crevices and cracks in rock. Some areas contain more groundwater than others.

An aquifer is an underground area that contains enough water for people to access it with a well. Aquifers are refilled by rainwater and melting snow as well as drainage from rivers and streams.

In fact, there is more clean, usable water to be found deep in the ground than in the earth's surface sources.

Groundwater is naturally cleaned and filtered through the soil and rocks around it. But if an aquifer becomes polluted, it is very difficult and expensive to clean up.

Serious problems can occur if there is a drought or a city draws water more quickly than rain and snow can replace it. Not only will there be a water shortage, but the land can actually sink!

Mexico City, the capital of Mexico, has sunk as much as 33 feet (10 m) in the last century. As the population exploded, the city drew too much water from the aquifer and kept drilling deeper and deeper to access it. Sidewalks and even schools have crumbled and caved in. Some buildings lean like a carnival fun house.

Groundwater is also used by bottled-water companies, which often pay little to access this public resource.

Some people claim bottled water is safer and healthier to drink than water from the tap. But in most places with managed water systems, this isn't true at all. Tap water in Calgary, Alberta, is tested 150,000 times a year — that's more than 400 times a day!

A bottle of water also costs up to two thousand times more than the same amount of water coming from a tap, requires two thousand times more energy to produce and uses more water in the production process than an average bottle can actually hold!

Plus, 91 percent of all plastic, including those water bottles, never gets recycled. Instead, it ends up choking landfills, fresh water and oceans.

As water shortages occur all over the world, people are beginning to understand how important it is that we preserve fresh water for people, not for profit.

After all, access to water is a basic human right.

Traveling from its source, water flows through rivers and streams and under the ground. But sometimes it needs help to reach our cities. Inspired by the Romans, engineers have created new aqueducts to harness the power of gravity.

Aqueducts today are largely underground pipes and tunnels as well as some aboveground canals and ditches that guide the water where it is needed.

The aqueduct system that transports water from the Sierra Nevada mountain range to the dry coastal city of Los Angeles, California, extends about 444 miles (714 km) — that's a seven-hour drive!

Before the journey from source to city is complete, water is often captured in a series of dams and reservoirs on the urban outskirts. By confining water in this way, a city can make sure the flow and supply are dependable. Dams on some reservoirs are used to generate electricity.

But reservoirs don't always work as planned. When Cape Town, South Africa, was hit by the worst drought in a century, its main reservoirs nearly went dry. Extreme conservation measures, including water limits of 13 gallons (50 L) per person per day — that's the equivalent of flushing a toilet four times — fixing leaky pipes and slowing the flow to a trickle have helped.

Still, scientists looking at the future of our warming planet suggest Cape Town is only the first of many cities that will need to find ways to conserve water.

Water is treated before it reaches our taps to make sure it's clean enough to drink. Most cities have treatment plants where water is cleaned in several steps.

First sticks and leaves, garbage and any other large matter must be removed.

Then chemicals are added that cause large particles — like clay, silt or algae — to bind together and settle to the bottom of the treatment tank.

The water is filtered through sand, gravel or charcoal to remove smaller particles such as dust, parasites, bacteria and viruses.

The next step is disinfection. Chlorine — the chemical used to keep swimming pools clean — is commonly added to the water because it quickly kills harmful bacteria, parasites and viruses.

Many cities in Europe and Asia purify water with ozone, which also removes unpleasant tastes and odors. Some cities, including New York, New York, and Winnipeg, Manitoba, use ultraviolet-light treatment as a second layer of disinfection.

Fluoride is sometimes added to the water to help prevent tooth decay.

Most of us think of salt water as undrinkable. But people have been turning salty ocean water into fresh drinking water — a process known as desalination — for centuries.

Until recently, desalinating water on a large scale was considered too difficult because it is expensive and uses a lot of energy.

There are also environmental concerns, since taking water from the ocean can result in harming or killing small fish and other organisms. The salt and chemicals removed from the desalinated water must also be handled carefully, as simply dumping this concentration back into the ocean can further endanger sea life.

But in the last few decades, many coastal areas from California to the Middle East have invested in more efficient desalination plants, and they are testing solar energy to power them. Engineers are also working on new technologies to deal with the salty by-products so marine life isn't harmed.

Filtered, disinfected and clean, water passes through large pipes beneath the city, headed toward homes and schools. A pressurized system of pumps and valves ensures there's enough power to keep the water moving.

Some of these pipes — called watermains — are so big that an adult could stand up straight inside! They become smaller, like the branches of a tree, as they turn into service pipes supplying water directly to homes and businesses.

Most of this vast grid of water pipes is under the sidewalks and roads. But in remote cities in the Far North, the ground is permanently frozen and water must be delivered to people's homes by truck.

Some cities store treated water in aboveground reservoirs, water towers or tanks.

All over North America, cities boast about their unique water towers, with shapes ranging from a watermelon to a teapot to a bottle of ketchup! Mostly, the towers are for storage, but they also help with water pressure and maintaining constant flow.

Tall city buildings also store water in their own tanks so that people have access (and strong pressure!) on the upper floors. Between ten and twenty thousand water towers dot the tops of buildings in New York, New York.

23

The average Canadian uses about 58 gallons (220 L) of water at home every day — that's about 700 glasses' worth! In the US, the number is even higher, at 88 gallons (333 L) per day.

Aging, leaky watermains can cost cities millions of dollars every year in wasted water and repair costs. Most cities haven't spent the money on maintenance that these complicated water systems require.

In houses and apartments, leaky pipes and faucets can also cost a lot of money and waste water. A pipe with a hole the size of a small pea will lose more than 8,454 gallons (32,000 L) of water a day. That's enough to fill 320 bathtubs!

Sometimes the water coming out of people's pipes and faucets — even in wealthy, developed nations — is not safe or clean.

Some years ago, residents in Flint, Michigan, began noticing that their water was brown, orange or red. It also tasted and smelled terrible. Then kids started getting rashes, and people lost their hair.

It turned out the water was tainted with lead, which can affect children's development and result in behavioral issues and learning problems.

Though government officials now call the water safe, many people in the city remain fearful and do not want to drink from their own taps.

In Canada, residents of at least one hundred First Nations communities have also lived with unsafe water for many years.

The reasons are complex and reflect the long and troubled relationship between the Canadian government and Indigenous Peoples.

Some communities have been told that their water shouldn't be used at all; others are instructed to boil it before use. Families report stomach troubles and skin problems related to contact with the water.

The Canadian government has made a commitment to end long-term drinking water advisories and improve water and wastewater systems on First Nations reserves. But many people remain worried, frustrated and angry.

Have you ever noticed that water in one city tastes and even *feels* different from water in another?

Taste is determined by where the water comes from and the minerals and other elements it comes into contact with in its journey to your glass. If it passes through limestone, it might taste slightly chalky or minerally. Water that comes from certain rivers or lakes can have an earthy taste. The amount of chlorine used for disinfection can also affect the flavor.

In Paris, France, there are drinking fountains all over the city that offer sparkling water!

As for the feel, people talk about "hard" and "soft" water, which is strange considering it's a liquid. Hard water has minerals in it, mostly calcium and magnesium. Soft water is often treated to reduce the mineral content so it is less damaging to plumbing and pipes. You know water is soft if it seems to take extra time to rinse away soap.

The urban water system doesn't stop once you've drained the sink or had a shower. Pipes in the walls and under floorboards in our homes, schools and businesses carry the water out to the street.

Some buildings have recycling systems to collect lightly used water from sinks, dishwashers, washing machines, showers and baths. Known as graywater, it's cleaned and treated onsite, then sent straight back for use in toilets and garden taps. These systems can reduce water usage and cost by almost half.

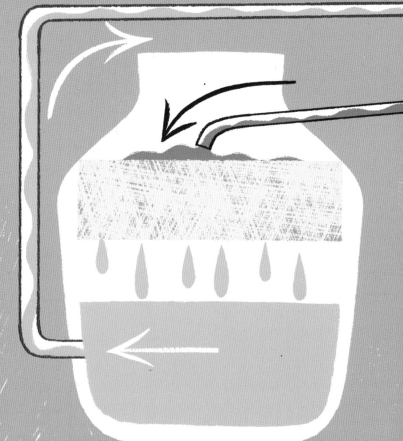

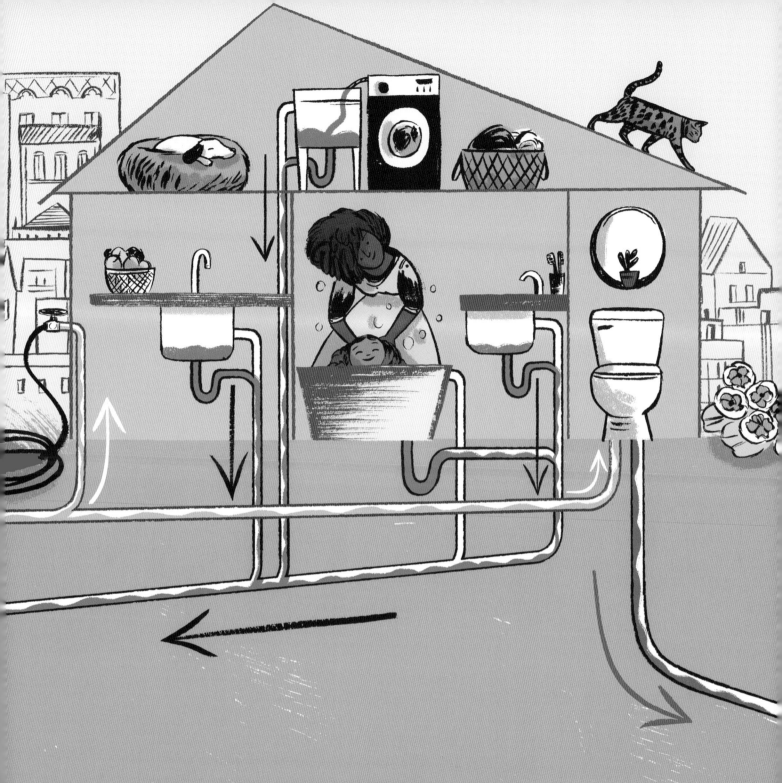

But in most homes, used water is flushed down the drain into a wastewater system below the streets. This sewer stream is about 99 percent water and less than 1 percent waste — things like food, toilet paper and poop.

As recently as 1940, in cities such as Boston, Massachusetts, and Pittsburgh, Pennsylvania, wastewater was dumped untreated into a nearby ocean, lake or river. This polluted the waterways and made people sick.

Today, cities direct wastewater toward treatment plants where it is filtered and cleaned, the solids and liquids separated. Then the wastewater is carefully treated and disinfected again.

Much of the solid matter is burned or taken to landfill. But, increasingly, cities see it as a resource. In Toronto, Ontario, some of the treated solid matter is made into fertilizer pellets that are used to help farmers' crops grow.

Scientists are also working on ways to separate metals from the sludge. Microscopic particles of gold, silver and other elements found in detergents, hair-care products and in waste from industry and electronics are flushed down the drains.

In fact, there could even be a fortune down there. In every city of a million people, there's at least $13 million worth of metal in the sewage!

Rain and snowstorms sometimes pound the streets with such force that water systems can't handle it, and roads and buildings flood.

In some cities, parts of the stormwater and wastewater sewers are combined, and rain or snowfall can cause polluted water to overload the system. Storms can also cause polluted runoff — from roads and parking lots as well as farmers' fields — to pour into the environment.

Scientists predict the earth will experience more intense storms as a result of climate change. Cities are responding by planting trees and reestablishing parks and wetlands, because green spaces can help soak up stormwater and prevent flooding.

In Shanghai, China, planners are creating a "sponge city," including 4 million square feet (400,000 sq m) of rain gardens and green roofs on top of buildings.

Other cities are managing stormwater by uncovering and cleaning up rivers that were long ago encased in sewers. These lost rivers are being "daylighted" in Seoul, South Korea, and Sheffield, England, making the cityscapes more beautiful, absorbent and better able to meet the demands of a changing planet.

Cleaned and treated, city water can be returned to the natural environment, usually a nearby lake or river, where it begins the cycle again.

But sometimes power outages at the treatment plant or excess water from a storm can result in raw sewage being released into the waterway. Canadian cities report that more than a trillion liters of raw sewage have spilled or leaked into lakes, rivers and oceans over a recent five-year period.

Treatment plants also struggle to filter out unexpected or new substances. For example, scientists have detected traces of people's medications in treated water.

Microplastics — tiny plastic particles in some products and clothing — can also pollute water and harm marine life. Canada and France have banned the sale of toiletries containing these plastic microbeads.

In other cities, including Sydney, Australia, some treated wastewater isn't discharged into the waterway at all. Instead, it is used for irrigation of sports fields, golf courses and farmland, as well as for dust control.

In Windhoek, Namibia, wastewater is treated so thoroughly that it is not sent back to a natural water source. Instead, it is drinkable straight from the plant. It's a new idea, and some people find it hard to accept. But as cities around the world face shortages, such recycled water is likely to become more common.

Access to clean, fresh water makes our cities work. It affects everything in our lives.

Drinking water keeps our brains healthy and our energy levels high. Simply hearing the sound of water bubbling and burbling can boost a person's mood and reduce stress.

Water also has an impact on important issues such as education, poverty and inequality. Without clean water, people in cities can't grow food, build housing, stay healthy or go to school. When water is scarce, it can also cause conflict between people and nations.

As the climate changes and populations grow, the health of the water on this planet we share is at risk. That's why even those of us in cities with clean, plentiful water must conserve now and preserve it for the future.

We are all part of the water cycle. And we can all play a role in caring for this precious resource.

Water is life. Jump in!

Make WAVES!

Help ensure our water remains fresh, clean and accessible to everyone.

What can we do to help?

- Turn off the tap when brushing your teeth and save up to 8 gallons (30 L) a day!
- Fix a dripping tap. Save over 300 gallons (1,136 L) of water a year.
- Take shorter showers.
- Ask your parents or school to install low-flow toilets and low-flow showerheads.
- Always carry a reusable water bottle, and avoid bottled water.
- Only wash a full load of laundry or dishes.
- Harvest rainwater for use in the garden.
- Plant drought-resistant flowers and plants in your garden, and don't water the grass!
- Encourage tree planting and the cultivation of green spaces.
- Choose alternatives to salt to melt ice and snow on your sidewalk.
- Join a community-based water monitoring group to advocate for and protect clean water. Check out waterkeeper.org.
- Always check the label for microplastics before you purchase personal-care products (see beatthemicrobead.org). You can also install a washing machine filter to prevent microplastics in clothing from getting into the water system.
- Never flush unused medicine down the drain or toilet. Many pharmacies have take-back programs.
- Energy conservation leads to water conservation, since water is often used to create electricity. Turn off lights, wash laundry in cold water, and use air conditioning and heating sparingly.
- Research the watershed connected to your city. Is it being preserved? Write letters to your local representative pushing for its protection.

Glossary

Algae: small organisms without roots or stems that grow in water.

Aqueduct: a channel for conveying water, whether underground or by bridge or canal.

Aquifer: an underground layer of rock, sand or gravel that contains water.

Chlorine: a chemical that is added to water to kill harmful germs.

Conservation: the protection of valuable things, especially forests, water and other natural resources.

Deforestation: the act of clearing forests so the land can be used for another purpose.

Desalination: the removal of salt from seawater.

Developed nation: a wealthy and technologically advanced country in which most people's basic needs for food, shelter, education, health care and income are met.

Drought: a long period of very dry weather.

Fertilizer: a substance, either natural (such as animal manure) or artificial, used to make soil more productive.

Fluoride: a chemical compound added to water to prevent tooth decay.

Graywater: the relatively clean wastewater from baths, sinks, washing machines and dishwashers.

Groundwater: the water that exists underground in the soil or in cracks and crevices in rock.

Microplastics: extremely small pieces of plastic debris in the water or environment that result from the breakdown of products or waste.

Ozone: a form of oxygen (made up of three oxygen atoms) that is used to kill bacteria and viruses in water.

Reservoir: a natural or artificial holding area for storing a large amount of water.

Runoff: the water and other substances that have drained away from the surface of land, buildings or other structures.

Sewage: liquid and solid waste carried away in sewers and drains.

Sewer: a system of underground pipes that carries away liquid and solid waste.

Ultraviolet-light disinfection: a water-treatment system that uses ultraviolet-light to damage viruses and bacteria at a cellular level so they are not able to grow.

United Nations: an international organization aimed at maintaining peace, security and human rights, as well as delivering aid to nations in need, promoting sustainable development and upholding international law.

Watermain: a large main pipe in a system of pipes that carry water.

Watershed: the area from which water is collected and drained toward rivers, marshes, streams and eventually larger bodies of water; also known as a drainage basin.

Selected Sources

Many sources were used to research this book. Here are a few that teachers and students might find helpful for further investigation. Don't forget to consult your city's website to find out more about how water is handled where you live.

canada.ca/en/environment-climate-change/services/
  water-overview.html
cdc.gov/healthywater
environmentaldefence.ca
epa.gov/watersense/watersense-kids
unwater.org
watercalculator.org
waterkeeper.ca
watersheds101.ca
wateruseitwisely.com/kids
water.usgs.gov/edu
worldwaterday.org

These illustrated books about water and the water cycle can offer further insight.

Banyard, Antonia & Ayer, Paula. *Water Wow! An Infographic Exploration.* Annick Press, 2016.
Mulder, Michelle. *Every Last Drop: Bringing Clean Water Home.* Orca Books, 2014.
Woodward, John. *Water.* DK Publishing, 2009.

Acknowledgments

I am grateful for the time and insights of Keith Brooks, Programs Director at Environmental Defence, a leading environmental advocacy organization, as well as Anton Meier at the University of Toronto. This book would not be possible without the smarts, patience and enthusiasm of Nan Froman, Emma Sakamoto, Semareh Al-Hillal, art director Michael Solomon, illustrator Katy Dockrill and the other dedicated superstars at Groundwood Books.

Precipitation

the Water Cycle